D0427115

FAMILY

FAMILY

The Real Measure of Success

TIM & BEVERLY LAHAYE

New Leaf Press

TIM &
BEVERLY
LAHAYE

THE
HEARTH
AND
HOME
SERIES

First printing: March 1998

Published in association with the literary agency of Alive Communications, Inc., 1465 Kelly Johnson Blvd., Ste. 320, Colorado Springs, CO 80920.

ISBN: 0-89221-370-1
Library of Congress Number: 97-75865

Cover by Left Coast Design, Portland, OR.
Interior illustrations by Pamela Klenczar.

Introduction

Two months ago I went golfing with my sons, Larry and Lee. We had a great time even though Larry, who golfs a lot and is a pretty fair player, beat Lee and I quite badly. As we were saying goodbye Larry gave me a big hug and said, "Dad, this has been the most fun game of golf I've ever had." Lee hugged me and said the same thing.

I wouldn't take a billion dollars for that moment and for what it says about our relationship. God has blessed my life with many gifts and honors — they all pale in comparison to the love I have for my two sons and two daughters. And frankly, I think that is the dream of every father and mother. Kids you love, are proud of, and enjoy being with. Who could ask for anything more of life?

The principles for good family living found in this book were first worked out for ourselves from the Scripture. Then I

presented them to the growing church we pastored in San Diego for 25 years. Then I started getting invitations to share them with other congregations, so I started Family Life Seminars — but basically I presented the same basic concepts in two-day seminars to over one million people.

Now you can get the same benefits by reading this book. I pray it will have the same effect on you it did on us and the thousands who testify that it helped their marriage and family. I know the principles work, for they come right out of the Bible.

— Tim LaHaye

Family: The Real Measure of Success

We often hear of programs, techniques, and "gimmicks" that will help us keep our families on firm footing. Sadly, these paths can lead to frustration rather than fulfillment for families because root issues aren't addressed. The heartbeat of the Bible is compassion, but many times, God's Word stands in the "tough love" camp.

In this section, Beverly LaHaye talks to wives about how God wants them to relate to their husbands.

When Tim was a young pastor, people often came to him with their problems. During the counseling session it would come out that they had already seen a professional counselor or psychiatrist.

"If you've been to a professional, why have you now come

to see me?" Tim would ask.

They always had the same answer, "Because I ran out of money, and I know you're cheap."

Tim quit asking that question and decided instead to be thankful for the opportunity to point them in the right direction.

Today, Americans have access to all kinds of self-help books, tapes, and seminars. The professionals are out there ready to give their latest spin on how to be happily married and have a happy home life. All they have to offer, however, are suggestions.

The Bible, on the other hand, provides authoritative principles that have passed the test of time. After all, where did the concept of "family" originate?

It was God's idea. Our Heavenly Father performed the first marriage ceremony in the Garden of Eden and instituted the first family.

If God created the family, wouldn't He have the best advice on how a husband, wife, and children can live together in harmony?

The apostle Paul, in writing to the believers at Ephesus, succinctly provides a synopsis on successful Christian family living. In fact, Ephesians 5:18-6:18 presents the Bible's longest passage on family living.

The introduction to this passage in Ephesians deals with the Spirit-controlled life. What does that tell us? That instruction on the Spirit-filled life was given for the family. If we can live the Spirit-filled life at home, we can live it anywhere. After all, what we are at home portrays what we really are.

Be Controlled by the Holy Spirit

When you accept Jesus as your Saviour and make Him Lord, the Holy Spirit takes control of your life. In fact, we are commanded to "be filled with the Spirit" (Eph. 5:18).

How are you going to be different now that you are filled with the Spirit? These verses from Ephesians summarize how you will be changed once the Holy Spirit takes charge of your life:

> Speaking to one another in psalms and hymns and spiritual songs, singing and making melody in your heart to the Lord, giving thanks always for all things to God the Father in the name of our Lord Jesus Christ, submitting to one another in the fear of God (Eph. 5:19-21).

You'll have a song in your heart, thanksgiving in your soul, and a submissive spirit in all your relationships.

We are to submit ourselves to one another, to fellow believers in the body of Christ. Serving one another in love becomes our goal in life. Instead of the selfish attitude that once ruled our lives, we now ask, "How can I best help someone else?"

What a contrast to the attitude found in our society today, where most people ask, "What's in it for me?" Even couples entering into marriage often do so with selfish expectations, "What am I going to get out of this?" or "What can he do for me?"

Jesus taught us to be servants, and Scripture commands us "to serve one another" (Gal. 5:13). Instead of focusing on ourselves, we, as Christian wives, should be putting others first — especially at home.

Marriage is not a two-way relationship; it's a three-way relationship. When God is left out, the relationship loses its most stable leg.

Before a marriage begins to fall apart, inevitably one or both partners have already thrown God out.

When the spiritual damage is repaired — and God is restored to His rightful place — then the couple has the divine resources to rebuild their marriage relationship.

Wives, Submit to Your Husbands

A well-known educational leader once told a group of college women that being a housewife is "an illegitimate profession." Women should "get out of the house and not be burdened with their children," she said. "Develop a profession, a career, so you can really make something of yourselves."

"Woman should not be under the leadership of the man," the feminists have insisted. "She should come out from under her husband's authority and be her own person." God's Word, however, makes it clear that He planned it differently:

> Nevertheless, neither is man independent of woman, nor woman independent of man, in the Lord. For as woman came from man, even so man also comes through woman; but all things are from God (1 Cor. 11:11-12).

While the woman is unique, with special physical characteristics, talents, wisdom, discernment, and emotions, God never intended for a wife to be her own person. God created her with these wonderful attributes to fulfill her required role as a helpmate for the man, her husband. The most fulfilling way for a woman to use her God-given gifts is within the secure boundaries of the marriage relationship.

Although the word "submission" has gotten a bad rap, it should carry a positive, not a negative meaning for women.

The fact is: Men need help! God knew it, and He created women to help them. That does not make women second-class citizens; it make us God's instruments to fulfill a particular role that helps keep God's creation running smoothly.

Whenever a wife thinks she can switch roles with her husband, God's original design gets distorted. The result? A marriage in conflict and a family in chaos.

Wives, submit to your own husbands, as to the Lord. For the husband is head of the wife, as also Christ is head of the church; and He is the Savior of the body. Therefore, just as the church is subject to Christ, so let the wives be to their own husbands in everything (Eph. 5:22-24).

The woman was designed and fashioned by God to make the husband a complete person. When husbands and wives walk together in unity, they help one another become better than either would have been without their mate.

Many women get hung up on "Wives, be in submission to your own husband," — and fail to see the most important part of this verse: "as to the Lord." When a wife comes to Jesus Christ, she submits herself to the Lord, knowing He will lovingly lead and care for her. In the same way, a wife can

willingly submit to her husband.

A godly Christian husband will have the mind of Christ. "For the husband is head of the wife, as also Christ is head of the church; and He is the Savior of the body (Eph. 5:23).

God's Word does not change. Jesus Christ is "the same yesterday, today, and forever" (Heb. 13:8). The Christian woman who wants her life to be grounded on an unchanging foundation will not balk at this teaching.

My work as president of Concerned Women of America has brought me into contact with women from all walks of life, including many feminists. I have had the opportunity to observe these women on a personal and professional level and have found most feminists to be frustrated and hurting women.

Rejected, disappointed, and heartbroken, they often project their bitterness and resentment onto others. Unfortunately, this is the only way they know how to respond. Searching for love and freedom, they flounder, having refused their only hope for peace and fulfillment in this life. I urge you not to be deceived by the world's empty philosophy. It has nothing to offer us.

> Beware lest anyone cheat you through philosophy and empty deceit, according to the tradition of men, according to the basic principles of the world, and not according to Christ (Col. 2:8).

God has already laid out His perfect plan for men and women and the family. If you return to the Word of God, you will find the way to personal happiness and a successful home life.

Husbands, Love Your Wives

Many women have had their homes torn asunder, or been rejected and experienced great disappointment, because their husbands did not know how to love. I have often wondered if there would be fewer feminists if they had married husbands who truly loved them "as Christ loved the church."

> Husbands, love your wives, just as Christ also loved the church and gave Himself for her. . . . So husbands ought to love their own wives as their own bodies; he who loves his wife loves himself. For no one

ever hated his own flesh, but nourishes and cherishes it, just as the Lord does the church (Eph. 5: 25-29).

Most wives would find it easy to submit to a husband who projects the loving humility and spiritual strength of the Lord as described in these verses. Imagine being loved as Christ loved the Church! I don't know any women who resist that kind of commitment, affection, and devotion.

Every husband needs to read and re-read these verses to remind himself to love his wife more than he loves his body — by nourishing and cherishing her. As Christ presents the Church spotless, without wrinkle and blameless, so the husband is to build up his wife until he can present her in this manner. A beautiful picture indeed.

Accept the Uniqueness of the Marriage Relationship

Genesis 1 describes the origin of the family that began when God created man from the dust of the earth. Soon after this great creative miracle, God realized it was "not good for man to be alone." Man needed a helper — someone who would meet his needs and assist him in his journey through life.

Another Adam would not fit the bill, neither would a dog or horse or any other animal. God knew man needed a helper who would make Adam better than he could be on his own.

The second chapter of Genesis describes how God "fashioned" a woman taken from the man's rib. This newly created being, although different physically, psychologically, and emotionally, would fit the man like a hand in a glove. She was suitable for the man.

To emphasize the uniqueness of this man/woman relationship, the command was given: "For this reason a man shall leave his father and mother and be joined to his wife, and the two shall become one flesh" (Eph. 5:31).

In recent years, the simplicity and perfection of God's original plan for the family has come under attack and — in many homes — exists as a twisted and ugly mutation. The husband/wife relationship lost its uniqueness for many men and women when God's original command was rendered obsolete in modern society. Don't fall for that lie.

Accept and enjoy the uniqueness of the marriage relationship. There is nothing else like it. No other human relationship provides the intimacy and security of marriage. In a godly Christian marriage, you and your mate are free to be your best and to become all that God wants you to be. When that happens, everyone benefits — you, your mate, your children, and society in general.

Respect Your Husband

Tim once told me about a godly woman who was married to an alcoholic husband. Apparently, he stayed sober long enough to earn a living as a lawyer.

In spite of her husband's constant belittling of her faith, this woman raised four boys — and all of them graduated from Dallas Theological Seminary and entered the ministry.

One day Tim had the opportunity to meet this woman's youngest son and asked him, "What was it like growing up?"

"My dad ridiculed our faith and even tried

to talk us out of believing in Jesus Christ," the young man said.

"With that kind of resistance, how did all four of you end up in the ministry?" Tim asked. "What was the secret?"

"It was my saintly mother," he replied with a smile. "She was a respected Bible teacher who taught 700 women in a Bible study. But when my father would come home in a drunken stupor, she would go to the door and find him lying on the threshold. Many times he had thrown up all over his clothes. My mother would lovingly wash him off, put him into bed, and get him to sleep. She always treated him with dignity and respect and would never permit us to say anything bad about Dad. She always told us, 'Boys, he is your father.' "

These young men grew up to be like their mother, not their father.

Respect goes a long way in creating harmony in a home. That's why God gave us this command: "Nevertheless let each one of you in particular so love his own wife as himself, and let the wife see that she respects her husband" (Eph. 5:33).

If you want your husband to love you, you have to be careful how you act toward him. At all times, no matter how angry you get, always respect your husband, especially in front of your children. That means not criticizing him or tearing him down.

A husband who knows his wife loves and respects him will

never have to look anywhere else for approval or affection. If he knows he can trust you, he will be free to share his heart with you.

Many wives complain that their husbands won't communicate with them on a meaningful level. One reason could be that husbands need to know you will listen without condemnation and that you won't repeat what he tells you. Also, keep in mind that men in general are not big talkers. In fact, Gary Smalley has noted that women speak 25,000 words a day while men only use about 12,000 words.

My husband, Tim, likes to tell the story about the man who heard that his dad was dying. He wanted to talk to him before he passed away, but he arrived a day late. When his brother met him at the airport, the man said, "I'm so sorry I didn't get here before Dad passed on. Did he have any last words?"

The brother replied, "No."

"Why not?" the man asked.

"Mama was with him right up to the end," the brother explained.

Maybe if we, as wives, talked less and listened more, our husbands' communication skills would improve!

In this section, Tim LaHaye provides interesting insights.

Your wife's wants — and needs — are different from yours. Why is that? First, because she is a woman, and women don't think like men. Women are wired differently. Secondly, her temperament type is different from yours.

To explain the different types — phlegmatic, melancholic, choleric, and sanguine — let's study the various ways people drive a car. Suppose four men, all of different temperaments, are driving down a four-lane highway and approaching an intersection. If you're a phlegmatic, you start slowing down a mile before the traffic light. If you're a melancholic, you apply your brakes at just the precise time to stop as the light turns yellow. The choleric speeds up at the sight of a yellow light and runs through it. The sanguine doesn't even notice the traffic signal because he's too busy talking to the guy in the back seat.

The way you eat your food, how you relate to people, your educational goals, your career — all result from your temperament.

If you can identify your wife's temperament type, it will

help you understand how she thinks and why she does things a certain way. This will allow you to accept her as a unique individual. She is a reflection of her temperament, just as you are of yours.

Out of the 6,000 people I have counseled over the years, 4,000 of them had marital problems. In the process I learned a lot about both men and women, and I'm convinced that opposites attract. In fact, my wife and I are complete opposites when it comes to temperament.

From our house there are two ways to get to the airport. One time Bev and I had to drive separate cars to get a flight. As we drove out of our housing complex and onto the main street, my wife turned one way and I turned the other!

Of course, my way was faster!

Your wife's temperament will determine her priorities and what she wants from you. Don't be surprised if you find it confusing to fulfill her expectations. Since your wife's temperament may be opposite to yours, her expectations will naturally be different. Also, your priorities may not be the same as your wife's because priorities are determined by temperament.

That can be changed if you, as the husband, are willing to be the kind of man God wants you to be. As a man you come with a different set of spark plugs. Men have different needs. Once you understand God's role for you, however, you will be able to give your wife what she wants — and needs.

God's Word explains your responsibility as a husband:

> Husbands, likewise, dwell with them with understanding, giving honor to the wife, as to the weaker vessel, and as being heirs together of the grace of life, that your prayers may not be hindered (1 Pet. 3:7).

A Woman Wants to Be Respected

As a husband, you are to live together with your wife and honor her as "the weaker vessel." Where is she weak? In her emotions. That's why a man should never criticize his wife. Always honor her and build her up.

Some women, because of feminist indoctrination, have been brainwashed into thinking they have "come a long way, Baby." Feminists worship "self" and make self-assertiveness and self-

actualization their main objectives in life.

A young woman may enter marriage with a defensive "You can't tell me what to do" attitude toward her husband. The older a woman gets, however, the more dependent she becomes on a man. Unfortunately, the converse is also true. If a wife dominates her husband in the early stages of marriage, then he'll be dependent on her later. It will also be difficult for her to accept her husband as the head of their household.

Respect her as a person. Why? Because she will accept herself according to the amount of respect you give her. The woman you married needs to be accepted regardless of how different she is from you. It's up to you to set the standard by respecting those differences.

Once you start showing respect for your wife, you must also demand that your children respect her. Kids aren't perfect either, and they are not going to automatically respect you and your wife. That's why God gave the command:

> "Children, obey your parents in the Lord, for this is right. "Honor your father and mother," which is the first commandment with promise (Eph. 6:1-2).

> Honor your father and your mother, that your days may be long upon the land which the Lord your God is giving you (Exod. 20:12).

These are the only two commandments in the Bible given to children. You, as the husband, must enforce these commandments in your home. Obedience and honor are not options.

I know that kids go through periods of rebellion when they outright refuse to submit to your authority as parents. During one difficult episode, one of our children wanted to move out and live with another family. "They're nicer than you are!" he said bluntly. You can imagine how that made us feel.

As the head of the house, the husband must set the standard by the way he talks to his wife and by what he expects of the children: "You will respect your mother, and you will respect me, whether you want to or not!"

Never, never, never let your kids sass or mouth their mother. Do not, under any circumstances, allow your children to "talk back" or verbally defile your wishes with, "I don't have to do

what you say!" or "You're always on my back!"

Sure, it's easier to ignore such rude and challenging behavior with, "Well, he didn't really mean what he said," and refuse to correct the child. If you let it go, you are merely reinforcing the expressions of a rebellious heart.

At that point, you need to remind your child that he is disobeying God's command to "honor your father and mother." Then you should initiate the proper punishment in order to reinforce the fact that rebellion and disobedience will not be tolerated toward you or your wife.

When I was in fourth grade, I came home from school one day and said something smart-alecky and disrespectful to my mother. I don't remember what I said or why. I didn't realize that my dad was also home until I heard my name come flying out from the other room: "Tim!"

"Yes, sir?" I asked as I crept around the corner. My dad hadn't moved. His leg was still thrown over the arm of the chair. All he'd done was call my name.

"I want you to apologize to your mother for what you just said," he commanded. "And, young man, if I ever hear you speak like that to her again, there will be a hole in the wall just your size."

little red wagon

My mother died at 81, and I never spoke disrespectfully to her again. Why? My dad respected her and demanded that I respect her, too. What do you think that does for a woman? It makes her respect herself. And that's the greatest gift you could ever give your wife. My dad died when I was nine years old, but he taught me a lesson I never forgot — and one that I have taught to my own children.

A Woman Wants Love

Men want love in marriage, but love isn't as high a priority for them. Men are more sexually oriented, and that's natural and normal. A man's sex drive reaches its ultimate peak about the age

of 21, then gradually tapers off after he's about 121, and then drops out of sight.

I started chasing the girls in the second grad. Until this very day my most difficult spiritual battle takes place in my mind. I work at keeping my thoughts pure by submitting my will to Jesus Christ — and it is a constant battle. One thing that helps me is to replace every unacceptable thought with something wholesome, because in the final analysis the battle is really won or lost in the mind. As the Bible teaches, as a man "thinks in his heart — so is he" (Prov. 23:7).

When I was a young preacher, an older pastor assisted me at a graveside funeral one day. I was so impressed with this 81-year-old man of God that I wanted his advice. "Brother Trotter, I need to ask you a question," I said. "How old do you have to get before you become, you know, before you get over being sexually tempted?"

He looked up at the sky and replied, "Brother LaHaye, I don't know. You'd have to be a lot older than I am."

That isn't exactly what I wanted to hear, but I realized I wasn't alone and that it was up to me to keep my desires under control.

Let's face it: men are sexually driven. Women are, too, at certain times, but their cycle is different from ours. A woman is sexually driven only about four to six days a month. A man's drive is more basic — like 58 days a month!

Scientists, in an effort to understand the difference between the sexual responses of men and women, attached electrodes to various participants. Then their emotional reactions to different pictures were measured.

When a man was shown a picture of an athlete, his response slightly increased. A photo of a Corvette sent the scale up much higher. A school textbook produced a negative response. But when a picture of a bikini-clad woman appeared, nearly every man's response went off the chart!

The women were given a similar test. A picture of a nice home with a white picket fence caused a very positive emotional reaction. A photo of a woman cooking in the kitchen caused a slight response. When shown a photo of a well-built man, her emotional level dropped. A picture of a baby, however, sent her emotional response skyrocketing.

Women aren't sexually driven; they are motivated by love. They don't just want sex. Oh, sure, they enjoy it and even desire it once in a while, but sex doesn't drive them like it does us men. Many times a good wife will co-operate in sex because what she really wants is love. And that's what God wants you to give her — love!

Husbands, regardless of your temperament type or how old your wife is, my best advice to you is: Love her, love her, love her. Let her know that you love her as a person and that the person who inhabits her body is more important than the body.

When one of our church deacons and his wife celebrated 56 years of marriage, Bev and I stopped by their house to congratulate them. Unable to have any children, they cherished one another with an unusual and endearing love.

During our visit, I noticed an old, yellowing photograph taken of the wife on her wedding day. Pointing to the picture, I said, "Frank, your wife was a beautiful woman."

"Yes, Pastor, she was." Then a warm smile crossed his face, and he said, "But she's more beautiful to me today than she was back then."

I looked at that picture, and I looked at the elderly woman, and, I'll be honest, I couldn't see what he saw. Why? Because I was looking at the outer shell, her physical appearance, and he was looking at her heart. It was that inner woman that he loved, and he had always made her feel that she was the most wonderful woman in the world.

USA Today proposed this question to wives: "If you had it to do all over again, would you marry the same man?" Fifty-one percent said no. When men were asked the same question, 77 percent replied, "Yes, I would marry her again."

Then the wives were asked a second question: "Does your husband help you voluntarily around the house?" Out of the 49 percent who said, "Yes, I would marry the same man again" — 82 percent responded, "Yes, my husbands helps out."

Were these wives more happily married because they had extra help at home? I don't think so. It was their husband's expression of love shown through his helpful actions that made the difference. Husbands, if you want to please your wife, find out what she hates to do around the house — and do it for her.

You know what my wife hates to do? She hates to empty the

dishwasher after the dishes are clean. In fact, Bev will let the dirty dishes pile up before she'll bother to unload the dishwasher and put the clean dishes away.

When I see dirty dishes accumulating in the sink and on the counter, I make a point of unloading the dishwasher for her. Nothing pleases my wife more than to open the dishwasher and find it empty so she can start filling it up again. That's my simple way of saying, "I love you."

Men, you'll find that it doesn't take much to please your wife, especially if you do something without her having to ask you. One act of lovingkindness can speak a volume of "I love you's."

Since Bev has arthritis in one of her shoulders, pushing the vacuum cleaner is difficult for her. As for me, I hate vacuuming because my mother always made me do it when I was a kid. My aversion to vacuuming, however, has been replaced by the pleasure I get in seeing my wife's face light up when she walks into our condo, opens the door, and notices the clean carpet.

Of course, I've learned to make my efforts obvious by leaving wheel marks. After all, if I'm going to go it, I might as well let it show!

Your love, expressed in words and deeds, makes your wife feel good about herself as a person. And when she feels loved and accepted, she no longer has to demand your affection and attention. Men are different. We can find our self-acceptance in other areas.

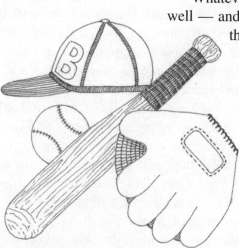

Whatever your job, if you do it well — and your boss pats you on the back and, particularly, if he gives you a raise, you feel good about yourself because men are vocationally oriented.

Athletics also boosts our self-esteem. That's why men can't resist a backyard game of football — even if it

means risking life and limb. Some men keep trying to be a stud at 30 and 40 and 50 when they should give it up. There's something about physical activity that builds us up as a man.

Fatherhood had a huge impact on our sense of manliness. Simply fathering a child, however, doesn't make a man a good father.

What makes a woman feel good about herself? Her husband. She receives her self-acceptance from you. If she feels only disapproval coming from you, she will be depressed and insecure. Even if she's the best lawyer in the town or the best doctor at the hospital, when your wife comes home she will feel inadequate if she senses your disapproval.

If you are a perfectionist, you probably have unrealistic expectations for your wife to meet. When she doesn't measure up to your impossible standards, you withhold your approval. Your wife will either drive herself crazy striving to be perfect or give up and live in a constant state of depression.

Men have a tendency to want to keep their

wives guessing. In some sadistic way, we think that keeps them on their toes. Actually, all it does is lower her self-esteem and make her feel insecure.

Remember, she is the "weaker vessel." Emotionally, she desperately needs to be constantly reassured that you truly love her — not just on your anniversary or Valentine's Day, but every day. As her husband, you must regularly communicate to her, "Honey, I love you so much that if I had it to do all over again, you would still be my first choice."

A Woman Wants Companionship

Your wife wants to become your best friend. I use the word "become" because it takes time. If you are a young married couple, don't be surprised if your wife isn't your best friend, yet.

I have found that Christian couples have a huge advantage in this area of marital friendship. Why? Because the husband and wife already share the most important bond between them — their faith in Jesus Christ. As a result, they have similar goals in life. Even if they have vastly different careers and interests, they share one overwhelming objective: to live a life pleasing to God. This puts Christian couples way ahead of the game.

Add to that the fact that their social and spiritual life usually revolves around the church. This is where they develop friend-

ships with other couples and participate in many activities together. The church and the overall Christian community provide an arena of commonality that bonds believers together as no other organization or social group can.

That doesn't mean that Christian couples agree on everything. I had a secretary at one time who was very conservative (she had to be to work for me). Her husband, however, was a liberal Democrat. They got along great until the elections rolled around.

During the Bush/Dukakis presidential election, their relationship was particularly strained. On election night, my secretary's husband was listening to the voting results on his way home from work. Dukakis was going down in flames, making him more and more depressed.

When he arrived home, his wife — overjoyed that George Bush was winning — walked over to greet him. "You're finally home," she smiled, waiting for her good evening greeting and kiss.

The guy looked at her and walked right by without saying a word. Stunned, she asked, "What's wrong?"

"I'm just not ready to kiss a Republican yet."

While some couples can allow for personal preferences and even dramatic differences of opinion, it doesn't make for smooth sailing. The more areas of commonality that a husband and wife share, the sweeter their marital friendship blossoms.

During the years when my wife spent most of her time caring for our four children, she had very little time to read books or articles. To make matters worse, she and I have different sleeping habits. Bev is an early-to-bed and early-to-rise person. I'm just the opposite — I do my best work at night and in the morning wake up like death warmed over. That fact alone could create serious problems in a marriage relationship.

As a minister, I was constantly reading and trying to keep up with the latest social and religious issues. In the evening, after dinner when the kids were in bed, my wife would fall asleep with a book in her lap. After all, it was 8:30 at night — twilight zone for Bev.

This went on for about ten years. She wasn't doing much reading, and I noticed that we were drifting apart mentally. We were no longer on the same wavelength.

Troubled, I began to pray about the situation, and God opened

my eyes. I noticed that Bev had an incredible memory. Whenever I told Bev about a book I had been reading, she could still recall it months later. I decided to begin sharing more information with her since she didn't have time to read herself.

One day I heard Bev explaining, almost word for word, to a friend facts I had long forgotten. I'm convinced she has a better memory than I do.

As a couple, you need to make sure you are both on the same page. If your wife is lagging behind, bring her along beside you. If your husband gets too far ahead of you, try to catch up. When you are on long drives together, listen to the same music or the same messages. Then discuss how the words or teaching applies to your lives and relationships.

If conversation is difficult for you, force yourself to ask your partner questions about their areas of interest — and if possible, to show you listen to their response, ask more questions based on what they have said. You will find this a handy way to improve common interests.

The more areas of commonality you can develop, the more you will enjoy each other's companionship. Your marriage will be enriched, and your friendship will grow.

A Woman Wants Protection

A minister friend was upset, "My wife lets the kids watch all kinds of garbage on TV."

I replied with a question: "Hey, what's wrong with you shutting the TV off? Maybe you should tell the kids, 'That's unacceptable in our family.' "

The husband should set the standard in the home.

As the physically smaller "weaker vessel," a woman wants to marry someone who's stronger and able to take care of her. She needs protection not only from personal harm but also from psychological damage.

Your wife and children need your protection — physically, emotionally, and psychologically. As the husband and father, you need to provide a decent income for your family, make sure the car is safe to drive, and keep the house in good repair.

Emotionally, you must listen to your wife's concerns and support her in any personal or family decisions. In addition, you need to weep when she weeps and rejoice when she rejoices.

A Woman Wants a Family

Most men also want children, but a wife *needs* a family. Before contraceptives and abortion, women didn't have much control over how many children they birthed. As a result, it was not unusual for a family to enjoy five, six — even ten children. Today, the average American family has only 1.6 children.

I often tell newly married couples, "Have as many children as you can raise to love and serve God." Why? Because the older you get, the more you realize that the most important thing in your life is your family.

Over the years, I have written 39 books (some are best sellers) and that gives me a tremendous sense of accomplishment. My greatest enjoyment in life, however, has come from our four children. Three are involved in Christian ministry.

Even today, Bev and I enjoy nothing more that being with our children and their families. In fact, we plan our schedules so we can spend vacations and holidays with some of the most important people in the world — our children and grandchildren. That's how important family is to us.

Cultivate your family by spending as much time together as possible. Learn to enjoy one another now, and you'll pave the way for many future years of happiness.

A Woman Wants a Leader

I once heard a story about a guy who dreamed he died and went to heaven. When he got there, he saw two doors. One was labeled, "You were the head of your family." On the second door was written, "Other." A long line of men were waiting to get inside that door.

The man walked up to door number one and was the first one in line. When the door was opened, an angel on the other side asked, "Why did you come to this door?"

The man replied, "My wife told me to." That man was probably married to a choleric — you know, the dictator type!

Every wife — no matter what her temperament — needs a husband who will take the lead and be head of their family.

If your wife has a choleric temperament, you may need to give her a little more room to express herself. If you impose your will arbitrarily, she will become totally frustrated. Give her the opportunity to give her opinion, but it is up to you as the husband to make the final decision.

I have a friend who was intimidated by his wife's strong will. When he came to me for counseling, I told him "Let your wife express herself, thank her for her opinion, and then you decide what is best for the family. But don't squelch her need to verbalize what she thinks."

Most women want a man who is going to lead. In the ideal situation, corporate decisions are made in which you decide together what to do in a given situation. Usually, however, one mate has to submit to the other partner.

When someone has to be the decision maker, it should be the husband. That's your job; it goes with the territory. You won't always be popular, but in the long run, even if your wife and kids disagree with the decision, they will respect the fact that you were man enough to make it.

As a father, I had to make many difficult decisions. The major ones I submitted to God, and the results were positive. On the minor decisions, I thought, *I can decide this myself*—and those were my biggest mistakes. Fortunately, God is a master at picking up the pieces and putting them back together again.

At 15 years of age, during a Christian summer camp, I gave my life to Jesus Christ for the gospel ministry.

Later I became enamored with becoming a lawyer, so I tried bargaining with God. "If you let me go to law school," I promised, "I'll come back and become the district attorney of Detroit and clean up the city."

God had other plans for my life, and I'm glad He led me into the ministry. It has not only been rewarding, it has been fun. God's will always turns out right.

Whenever you have to make a major decision in life, get alone with God and lay out your conditions before Him. Then pray, "Lord, this is what I'd like to do, but I know that You have a will for my life, and I want You to guide me to do the right thing."

When a difficult family decision — big or small — has to be made, pray for wisdom to judge the matter fairly. Then ask God to give you the strength to stand by your decision. The more unpopular the decision, the more graciously you need to present it to your family. Do it resolutely without backing down, no matter how much opposition you face. Remember, you are responsible to God to be the leader of your household.

During our family life seminars, I often suggest to those attending that they write down any questions they want me to answer. One of the top five questions — from among the hundreds that are asked every year — comes from wives who ask: "How can I get my husband to be the spiritual leader of our family?"

What is a spiritual leader? A man who is spiritually minded himself and who leads his family in spiritual growth. I hope you have a time, at least four or five days a week, when you lead your wife and children in family devotions. All it takes is ten minutes out of your busy day to read a small portion of Scripture and pray together about the needs of your family. By your example, you set the spiritual pace for your children to follow — whether it is prayer, daily Bible reading, or church attendance.

In addition to family-time prayer, the husband and the wife need to pray together concerning issues that affect you as a couple.

A few years ago, Bev was asked to appear before the Senate judiciary committee confirmation hearing for Judge Robert Bork. Naturally, she was very nervous. It must be pretty intimidating to speak for five minutes in front of well-known senators like Ted Kennedy, Joe Biden, and others.

As Bev was hurrying out of the house, I could tell she was nearly overwhelmed by the tremendous responsibility facing her. I took her in my arms and prayed for God to give her peace and wisdom.

Later, a federal judge in Asheville, Kentucky, who had come to a men's seminar where I was speaking, came to me afterward and asked, "Would you give a message to your wife? I caught her testimony at the judiciary committee for the appointment of Judge Bork, and I thought she did a superb job." Actually, she did a supernatural job because of the grace of God.

When your wife faces difficult situations that press her to the limit of her abilities and talents, you need to be there supporting her. That is not the time for an ego trip on your part. That's the time to act like a man, take her in your arms, and say, "I'm here for you, sweetheart. Let me pray for you. I know you'll do great!" Your wife needs to know that you support her spiritually.

A Woman Wants Happiness

Every person who has ever come to me for counseling had the same problem: They were miserable. I've never had anyone come in for marriage counseling and say "Pastor LaHaye, we are so happy we just can't stand it. Could you help us?"

No. It's always been the opposite. "We have made each other miserable." No one gets married to become miserable. Every bride thinks she has found Mister Right, and he is going to make her happy forever after. It doesn't work that way. All those people who needed counseling because they were miserable had one thing in common: They had earned the right to be miserable. Why? Because they had broken the principles of God.

More than once, a woman would tell me about this brute she married and how he's mistreating her. When I ask her why she married him, she says, "I married an unbeliever against my parents' wishes."

What's wrong with wanting happiness? Isn't that what we're here for? Every human being wants happiness, and as Christians we have the greatest resource on happiness in the world — the Bible.

Did you know that the word "blessed" really means happy? Jesus said, "I've come that you might have life and that you might have it" — how? — " more abundantly." Jesus makes everything more abundant.

I took a sex survey of 3,404 people and discovered that Christians have the highest level of sexual satisfaction and frequency than any other segment in our society. We don't brag about it, we don't talk about, we don't read dirty books about it, we just go on enjoying it year after year after year, better than any group in our culture.

The world has a twisted view of sex because they think that the physical experience on a human level is all there is to it. Chris-

tians, however, involve the spiritual part of our lives, and that enriches everything.

What is the secret to happiness? Jesus gave it when He said, "Blessed are those who hear the word of God and keep it" (Luke 11:28). "Blessed" is another word for happy.

As a husband and father, the head of your household, you need to make this commitment: *My family is going to follow Jesus Christ. We're going to obey the Word of God*. If you do that, you will be a happy husband with a happy wife and happy children.

I hope you'll invest yourself in the greatest institution in your life — your family.

In this section, Beverly LaHaye returns to Ephesians 6 for tips on family life and raising children.

One Sunday morning after church, a lady from our congregation came by and grabbed my husband's hand.

"Pastor," she begged earnestly, "would

you promise to pray for our family every day?"

"Why, Sylvia?" Tim asked.

"Our youngest child just turned 13," she moaned, "and I realize we now have three teenagers all at the same time!"

Tim was so impressed by her request that on the way home he told me about the incident. I turned and looked at him rather strangely. "Tim, don't you realize that we have four?"

A panicked look came across his face as he realized we needed more prayer support than Sylvia!

Every father and mother wants to be a good parent. But anyone who has children knows it isn't an easy assignment.

Where Should We Turn for Advice?

A Christian insurance man once told Tim, "I used to give Dr. Spock's books on childrearing to anyone who bought insurance or any clients who had a new baby."

Tim and I couldn't understand why until we realized that back in those days, there was very little teaching on raising children — or on marriage and family life in general.

After 30 years of teaching Spockism and permissiveness and "don't spank your children," Dr. Benjamin Spock himself, at 76 years of age, publicly announced on television, "I made a mistake. You should discipline your children. You

should teach them responsibility."

Guess what? The Bible has been teaching that for millenniums.

Let's go back to Ephesians 6 for instructions on how children and parents can live happily together.

Children, Obey Your Parents

Children, obey your parents in the Lord, for this is right. "Honor your father and mother," which is the first commandment with promise: "that it may be well with you and you may live long on the earth (Eph. 6:1-3).

Children need to be under the authority of their parents. They need our love, our guidance, our wisdom, and our protection.

At the same time, children need to honor their parents. In fact, as parents we do our children a favor by making them honor and obey us. Why? So they can enjoy the promises of

God. What could be better than for your children to have everything in their lives go smoothly? What greater gift than to have your child enjoy a full, rewarding, and long life?

Without proper training in respect and discipline, a child grows up without self-control or self-respect. This leaves him vulnerable to his own childish whims and desires.

Did you know that more teenagers today die in accidents of one kind or another than from any other cause of death? Suicide also ranks high on the death list. It's a dangerous world out there, and you do your child no favors by letting him do as he pleases.

My husband Tim relates an incident that makes this point quite well:

> One day, when I was 17 years old, my mother told me, "Tim, God spoke to me about you this morning in my devotions."
>
> I always hated to hear her say that. I remember praying, "Lord, quit sending messages by my mother. Send them direct."
>
> Then she pulled out her Bible and read. "Evil companions corrupt good morals," she quoted. "Son, I've come to the conclusion that those four boys you've been

running around with are having a bad influence on you."

I couldn't believe it. "But, Mom, you want me to break off with friends I've played sports with through junior and senior high," I complained. "If I do that I won't have *any* friends."

"Yes, you will," she said. "I want you to go down to the church and make new friends."

"I don't even like those guys. They're a bunch of sissies!" For the first time in my life, I defied my mother — who had been a widow since I was nine years old. Politely and respectfully, I said, "Mom, I won't do it. They've been my friends too long. I will not do it."

At just five feet tall, she pounded on the table with her bony little finger and said, "Young man, as long as you park your feet under my table, you will abide by my rules. You either break off with those friends or you leave home."

I left home — for two days. Nobody would feed me, so I came back.

My mother met me at the door and asked, "On my terms?"

"Yeah, Ma, on your terms."

Thank God, I had a mother who could see where I was headed. I would have destroyed myself. I later learned that one of those four former friends spent 16 years in the federal penitentiary. Two of them have been married and divorced three times.

As for me, I went on to serve the Lord as a pastor and marry a wonderful wife. I am what I am today because my mother had the courage to stand on God's Word and not back down in the face of my defiance.

By the way, some of my best friends today are the guys I met at the church.

Left to himself, a child will never have the inner strength and will power to resist peer pressure, drugs, alcohol, sex, or any other sin.

Back in 1979, during the International Year of the Child, we

first began to hear about "children's rights" and "the child advocacy laws." Secular humanists were advocating that children should have the right to sexual activity, to their own finances, and even the right to vote. Why? Because they are human beings.

Children in America today face issues that didn't even exist 20 years ago. As a parent, you must continuously be aware of how you can best meet your children's needs today — lest they be lost in the conflict.

Fathers, Don't Provoke Your Children

Fathers, do not provoke your children to wrath, but bring them up in the training and admonition of the Lord (Eph. 6:4).

In other words, Dad, don't be so unreasonable that your children become totally frustrated. Use common sense when you make your rules and decide on punishments. Treat your children the way you like to be treated. Don't use your position of authority over them to demean them psychologically or harm them physically. If you do, they will become exasperated and lose all respect for you.

The responsibility for training and discipline is given to fathers. Why? Because husbands who are also fathers are the head of the family and carry the responsibility for training and disciplining the children.

This does not mean that Mom should sit idly by and tell the child, "Wait 'til your father gets home!" It does mean that the wife enforces the rules and standards of discipline determined by her husband.

Families, Be Strong in the Lord

Since the apostle Paul has been talking about household

issues in Ephesians 5 and 6, it is reasonable to assume that Ephesians 6:10 is also addressed to family members.

The word "finally" tells us that Paul is summing up everything he has already said: "Finally, my brethren, be strong in the Lord, and in the power of his might."

Yet, what's happening in our society today? Families are torn apart, divorce rates increase every year, young people run away from home, children rebel against parents, and the family unit becomes weaker and weaker. Why? Because we've let down our guard.

How can we strengthen our families? By putting on "the full armor of God that you may be able to stand firm against the schemes of the devil" (Eph. 6:11). What is the "full armor of God"? God's Word.

You cannot raise children today, have a strong family, and resist all the schemes of the devil and society without the authority of the Word of God.

We are living in evil days. Children are

being pulled away from parental guidance and taught things which are contrary to God's Word.

America's public school system teaches our children to deny God as their Creator by presenting evolution as fact instead of theory. The schools have usurped parental authority in many areas, including the right of the parent to teach their children about proper sexual behavior.

As a parent, you need to re-stake your claim and stand your ground. Instill proper moral values and conviction in your children. Have regular times of family Bible study. Be strong in the Lord. Rescue your children from the enemy's clutches before it is too late.

Parents, Stand Firm against Sin

> Therefore take up the whole armor of God, that you may be able to withstand in the evil day, and having done all, to stand (Eph. 6:13).

Let's look at some specific areas where we, as Christian parents, need to take a firm stand.

• Drugs and alcohol.

I recently read an article about fourth grade children who

were becoming alcoholics and drug addicts. Why is this happening in our society? Some children are simply following their parents' example. Television also makes drinking look glamorous. Macho men take a beer can and crush it with their hands while lovely ladies hold martinis in their hand.

This one-sided view fails to present the harsh reality to children: Alcohol destroys lives and families. Television needs to show the broken homes, the mothers and children beaten up by alcoholic fathers, the child's wagon crushed by the roadside after being hit by a drunken driver.

Don't expect society to teach your children not to drink alcohol. You, as Christian parents, must take a firm stand against it and follow through with strict punishment if your child disobeys. Set the standard and enforce it with your teenagers. You may save his or her life if you do.

• X-rated movies and television programs. Immorality has flooded into America's living rooms. With one click of the remote, adultery, sexually explicit behavior, profanity, blasphemy — filth we would never tolerate in person — infiltrate our lives under the guise of sitcoms, humor, drama, and mystery.

Like a computer, our minds absorb everything we take in through our eyes and ears and stores it away in different files. Whenever a situation arises, that file comes up and influences how we will act at the moment.

If your children are watching hours and hours of sexually explicit movies and TV sitcoms, guess where that information is being stored. In their minds. And guess how they will act when a tempting situation arises.

Why do you think teen sex and teen pregnancies are so common? Because kids and teens have been programmed by what they see and hear to act and react accordingly.

It's up to you as a parent to take a strong stand against immorality, and the place to begin is in your own family room.

• The homosexual/lesbian agenda.

What is their agenda? To suck as many children as possible into their filthy pit.

Make no mistake about it. They are out to trap your children. They have already infiltrated the schools with explicit teaching about their "alternative lifestyle."

This so-called "gay" lifestyle has nothing to do with happiness. Sadness and heartache always result when anyone disobeys God's commands regarding sexual purity. AIDS and other sexually transmitted diseases have already taken a toll in America.

Most homosexuals were lured into this debilitating lifestyle because of a sexual encounter during childhood, and it was often with a friend, relative, or baby sitter.

Always know where your children and teenagers are and who they are with. You can never be too careful.

These are only a few of the temptations your children face on a daily basis. As adults, we have more freedom to remove ourselves from unpleasant or ungodly activity. Kids and teens, however, are bombarded by wickedness day after day. That's why you need to make your home a place of refuge. Monitor which programs your children watch on TV, refuse to allow rock music, get acquainted with their friends.

Taking a stand against evil is not easy. That's why the apostle Paul follows his admonition to "resist evil" with armor and weapons of warfare.

If you don't fight for your family, who will? You must take an active part in our children's defense. Unless you and I stand up and speak out against these sins in our society, as the Word of God teaches, our children or our children's children will certainly be overwhelmed in the enemy's wake.

Pray at All Times

When should we pray? "Praying always with all prayer and supplication in the Spirit" (Eph. 6:18).

Pray for your children, your husband, your wife. Pray for our nation, our schools, our government officials. Pray whenever you see evil gaining ground. Be on the alert against new attacks. Don't stick your head in the sand and pretend that the evil of our day will somehow vanish.

It takes courage and perseverance to build a strong family today, but it can and is being done in homes all across America.

Tim and I had the opportunity to meet Dr. Frances Shaffer before his death. This great man of God made a tremendous impact on his generation. He made a statement that will ring in our ears for years to come: "He that will not use his freedom to pre-

serve his freedom will lose his freedom, and neither his children nor his children's children will rise up to call him blessed."

Dr. Shaffer put those words into action. In his dying days — in fact, ten days before he succumbed to the cancer that was eating at his body — he picketed an abortion clinic. Why? Because he wanted to preserve the freedom of speaking out for the unborn children.

"Pay close attention to great men and women of God in their dying days," Dr. Shaffer told his children and grandchildren, "because very often their last words will be a great message that you must heed."

What were Dr. Frances Shaffer last words to his family? "Do not give up the fight; keep on praying; keep on fighting."

That's what God is saying to us as Christian parents today: "Keep praying and fighting for your family."

In this section, Tim LaHaye explains how humanism affects America's children and what you can do to protect them.

Where the Battle Rages

Why are Americans losing the battle for the family? Why is family life in such jeopardy today? The answers lies in the conflict between two major ideologies.

What Is Secular Humanism?

What is the most powerful philosophy in America today? Secular humanism. In fact, the only group capable of resisting the humanist onslaught are born-again Christians who know their Bible.

Based on the idea that "man is the measure of all things," humanism promotes these basic principles: atheism, no God, and evolution.

Educators and academicians love the theory of evolution. Why? Because it justifies man's origin without God. If they can explain away God, then they don't have to answer to Him, or so they reason.

What makes evolution so dangerous? If you teach a generation of people that they are animals, pretty soon they will start

acting like animals. And animals are universally amoral. They are not created in the image of God, as man is, nor do they have a moral consciousness.

Only the Bible teaches that man has an inborn conscience that either accuses or excuses us. If we do right, we feel good about ourselves. When we do wrong, we feel bad.

Why do people have a guilt neurosis? Because they're guilty. Only those who believe in the death and resurrection of Jesus Christ can confess their sin and be forgiven of it. Why? Because God's Word says, "If we confess our sins, He is faithful and just to forgive us our sins and to cleanse us from all unrighteousness" (1 John 1:9).

God removes our transgression as far as the east is from the west, and our sin will never again be remembered against us.

Neither Freud nor Skinner nor any humanist psychologist or psychiatrist can remove your guilt. All they can do is try to talk you out of it — after all, there is no right or wrong in their eyes. That's why so many people are depressed today. They have no way to resolve their feelings of guilt.

This puts kids in tremendous jeopardy, because young people, more so than adults, don't know how to handle their guilt. As a result, they sink into deep depression and many times never recover. This is one reason the suicide rate among teens is so high. They see no way out, and hopelessness eventually overwhelms them to the point of taking their own lives.

Trapped in the Sexual Revolution

At school and through the media, the humanists bombard children with blatant messages encouraging free sex.

"You need to learn how to use your bodies and practice your sexuality," kids are told, long before they are mature enough to bear the responsibilities of their deeds. "Don't worry about your parents. They're just old fuddy-duddies."

Parents want their children to be moral, but educators think they know best: "Bring in Planned Parenthood." Now there's a con job.

After decades of Planned Parenthood's influence in America's schools, what did we get? A teenage pregnancy rate that increases every year, making it the number one social problem in our nation today.

Add to that the lie of "safe sex," and what happens? An epidemic of AIDS and venereal diseases that is devastating a generation of young people like the plaque.

What is the natural result of this sexual revolution? Teaching amorality has corrupted a generation and destroyed family life in America. Chastity before marriage and faithfulness to one mate has become obsolete. Many kids today have never even heard those words.

When they do get married, they usually don't last. Why? Because all they've been taught is how to have sex — not how to build a marriage relationship. In fact, the most common marital destroyer today is infidelity, either physical or mental.

Anyone who indulges in sexual fantasies long enough will eventually act it out. Infidelity damages a marriage more quickly and more completely than any other sin. Why? Because marriage is a sexual contract. When two people become one, they pledge themselves, as long as they both live, to keep that contract. Such pledges mean little to a generation that has had no limits placed on sexual activity.

The American Mindset

People like to say that we live in a pluralistic society. As far as I know there are only two major plurals: secular humanist thought and the Judeo-Christian moral ethic.

Although our country was founded on biblical principles, the humanists, in the last century, have taken over the media, the government, the public school system, and a number of important organizations. As a result, a mere 10 or 15 percent of our population has a controlling influence on 90 percent of our culture.

The humanists have come along and said, "Anything goes. Make up your own mind. There's no one up there telling you what's right and wrong."

Man's wisdom centers around atheism, evolution, and amorality, because these theories put man at the center of his autonomous, self-centered worldview.

That's the mindset that many Americans have adopted. It's preached at us day after day, hour after hour — over the radio, in music, by the news media, in TV sitcoms and documentaries. Even the Discovery Channel, the Animal Planet, and Public

Broadcasting propagate the theory of evolution, and their belief that man is an animal.

The media has brainwashed an entire generation, and American culture is paying the price.

Circle the Wagons!

I've lived in Southern California long enough to know that most of the evils affecting our society emanate from Hollywood and permeate throughout the United States. We have a culture that is working insidiously to destroy the family.

With God's help, you can still have a happy marriage, a good family, and raise children to love and serve God — even in this hostile culture of ours. If that is your goal, however, you will need tremendous determination. If you don't make family living, marriage, and child raising your highest priority — and spend more time at it than your parents did — you'll lose your children.

And we are losing them. In the evangelical churches today, we are losing between 35 and 50 percent of our young people to the world before they graduate from high school. Why? Because of the cultural evils and the lack of protection around the home.

It's not too late. As parents, you can keep that from happening by building "rings of insulation" around your family to keep out society's insidious forces. It's time to circle the wagons.

Provide a Safe Refuge for Your Children

In American society today, it is nearly impossible to escape the barrage of humanist deception and lies.

Did you know that in the last 30 years Christianity has more than doubled in our country? In fact, church growth has almost tripled.

As Bev and I

travel across the United States, we find many large churches with hundreds of members where the Bible is being preached. People are being drawn to the truth, and the Holy Spirit is speaking to hearts and blessing families.

At the same time, the humanist influence on our culture has promoted a downsurge in moral values. We are closer to Sodom and Gomorrah today than we were 30 years ago. Why? Because Christians have abandoned the most influential arenas — the media, government, and secular education — the places where public opinion is formed.

There is a place of refuge. It's in your home and your church. Thankfully, Christian media — television, videos, radio, music — is becoming stronger and providing alternatives.

It's up to parents, however, to set the example by what you read, watch, and listen to. Then you can encourage your kids to do the same.

Get involved in your children's education. Home school them if necessary, or make the financial sacrifices necessary to send them to Christian school.

If your child has a humanistic education, his view of God, creation, mankind, and himself will be distorted. This will affect his goals in life and how he treats other people.

If your child has a biblically based Christian education, he will learn to value the principles of integrity, humility, service, and love taught by Jesus Christ.

An important, but often overlooked, way to protect your family and children's future requires your involvement in the political process. You need to be a registered voter, and you need to vote in every election of our governing official, from the local tax collector to the president.

Christians also have a responsibility to vote for people who share their moral values. Vice President Quayle, whom I know to be a born-again Christian, was right when he said we are in a great cultural divide between the elite in the media, education, and government. They are on one side, and the rest of America is on the other.

Most Americans — the vast majority — don't want to live in Sodom and Gomorrah, but that is exactly where we are headed if we don't vote the humanist agenda of the liberal left into extinction. We believe it is a sin against God, our family, our church, and our country for Christians to ignore their voting responsibilities.

Our Christian founding fathers gave us the greatest nation on earth, one that has provided more freedom to more people for a longer period of time than any other in history. Liberal secular humanists are destroying our once-Christian culture due to the apathy of the 52 percent of Christians who do not even vote.

I believe God will hold us accountable for our lack of Christian responsibility for not voting into office those who share our moral values. In a republic, we deserve the kind of government we get, by voting or not voting. The very least we can do for our children is try to vote into office men and women who make good moral role models.

Give Your Kids a Loving Home

Parents, I hope that you'll make every effort to love not only each other, but your children.

One tangible way to show your love is to reach out and touch them. Christian psychologist John Trent suggests that every child needs about 25 touches a day — and every partner, particularly every wife, needs at least 12 touches every day.

Men, don't wait until 10 o'clock at night and then give your touches all at once.

A touch is an identification. When you reach out to a child or your mate, you are saying, "You are special to me." As you pass by your son or daughter and gently touch his or her shoulder, you let that child know, "You are very special to me."

Love is like electricity — you can't see it, but you recognize the results of it. Love doesn't have to be expressed, but it's more enjoyable when it is. Take time to reaffirm your love.

Children who are loved grow up to have greater self-worth. If a young person comes from a broken home or from a love-starved family where they don't feel accepted, that affects how they view themselves.

I have a grandson who was born without an ear canal, making him totally deaf in one ear. The other ear had only a tiny ear canal. God mercifully answered our prayers and now he has 100 percent hearing in that ear.

He also has a rare defect that prevented his jawbones from growing. Every few years he goes in for surgery so the doctors can graft bone into his jaw to make him look normal. When his face begins to grow again, his jaw appears a bit out of proportion

until the next surgery. Now, as he prepares to go into his twenties, thanks to several surgeries he is a handsome young man.

When he was three and a half years old, we were having the LaHaye Christmas family gathering at our house. All the adults were sitting around the living room when he came down ready for bed. His parents told him to kiss all the relatives, so he went around and kissed four grandparents, his parents, his cousins, and their married partners.

This kid kissed 23 adults before he went to bed! No wonder he has a good feeling about himself. He thinks the whole world loves him! "I am important because 23 adults reached over and embraced me and made me feel like I am special." Today, he is a very secure, popular, and normal young man.

Our world is starving for love. Children have a natural desire to want to believe "My parents love me."

I was raised in a very poor family. My father died when I was nine years old, leaving my mother a widow with three little children. My brother was only seven weeks old at the time. Without any income, my mother had to trust God.

Financially, our family had some very grim years, but as I look back on my childhood, I think I was rich. Why? Because I knew what it meant to be loved.

You may have been raised in the lap of luxury, but if you didn't have love, you were cheated out of life's most important gift.

I look back and think, My mom and dad dearly loved me. I was important to them. That's the greatest gift you can give your children. Take time to love every member of your family each day.

Take Them to a Bible-Teaching Church

The church you attend is the best friend your family has. I have seen from experience that the strongest and the best families attend church. The church is the one organization in our culture that supports the values you are trying to inoculate into your children. Your church provides sound Bible teaching for the entire family, from the nursery children and primaries through junior high and high school.

Is church attendance necessary? Yes, if you want to obey

God's Word, which teaches us not to forsake "the assembling of yourselves together" (Heb. 10:25).

"But my kids are at that age when they don't want to go," you say. Take them with you anyway.

Some Christian families have an election on Saturday night. Are we going to go to church tomorrow? That's spiritual suicide.

Raise your kids with this understanding, "Unless you have a communicable disease that will endanger somebody else's health, we all go to church on Sunday." It isn't a matter of *you* go, it's *we* go.

In essence, you are saying, "Follow me as I follow Christ."

How to Have Happy Children

Hearing and doing the principles of God is the key to happiness. The principles of God are not only timeless, they work.

If I throw my pen up in the air, I know it will come down. Why? Because God the Creator designed a principle called the law of gravity.

The Bible teaches, "Children are a heritage from the Lord, The fruit of the womb is a reward" (Ps. 127:3) and "Happy is the man who has his quiver full of them" (Ps. 127:5).

Your children will be a blessing to you, if you raise them according to the principles of God. No one else is going to teach your children values except the church and the family. It is your responsibility to teach your family biblical principles to live by.

Teach Your Child That He Is Unique

Every child is unique and is born with a certain temperament. The temperament theory is based on the idea that we are born with a certain kind of temperament — the same way you are born with the color of your hair and eyes. If you are an introvert, you were born an introvert. And if you are an extrovert, you were born an extrovert. Temperament accounts for 20 to 30 percent of your child's behavior.

A few years ago, I was introduced to a psychologist, who blatantly asked: "Oh, you're the guy who speaks on temperament, aren't you?"

"Yes," I replied.

"I think that's a lot of bologna!" he quipped.

"Well," I replied, "last night I attended our church's pre-school Christmas program and made an interesting observation."

"Really?" the psychologist asked.

"When the little ones had assembled on stage, I noticed a little boy — I'll call him Johnny — in the back row, stretching his neck and looking over the faces in the audience. Finally, he spotted his dad and shouted, 'Hi, Dad!' as he waved and jumped in an effort to be seen.

"A little girl on the front row also caught my eye, same size and age as the uninhibited boy in the back row. Suzy shuffled to her place with downcast eyes. Obviously petrified by the crowd, she reached down for the little tassel on her dress, pulled it up, and put it in her mouth.

"Now, Doctor," I proceeded to ask, "do you mean to tell me that the different types of behavior exhibited by those toddlers was learned in only two years, or was it born in them?"

Fifty years from now, Johnny will still be outgoing and un-inhibited, but hopefully not obnoxious. And Suzy, although probably more sure of herself by then, will have retained her demure and reserved personality.

One young mother, whose toddler had an unmistakable choleric temperament, told me, "He gets into everything and won't sit still for a minute." When I asked her about his conduct in the womb, she answered, "He kicked every organ in my body!"

My mother said the same. Maybe yours did, too.

God blessed Bev and I with four children — a girl, two boys, and a girl. They are so different we often wonder if they are really ours! Although they were formed from the same gene pool, each one has distinct physical features and a unique temperament. And its something that came with them at birth.

Sometimes when parents introduce me to their son, I can't help but wonder, *Could this kid have come from these parents? He must be adopted.* Then at a later time, I will meet the boy's grandfather and realize, *This kid is a dead ringer for his granddad!*

No wonder. After all, we come from two parents and four grandparents, who have all contributed genes to our makeup, both physical and temperamental. At least six people, and maybe some great-grandparents, supply components of our nature.

Most people are a combination of two or more temperaments — a strong one and a secondary. Other factors also affect the way your child thinks and acts. Childhood training, habits, education, self-discipline, motivation, mental attitude, and health all affect his behavior.

In school, the Sparky Sanguine kid usually functions between D- and F, but still thinks he's Mr. Wonderful. Sanguines especially need to cultivate self-discipline.

The Melanie Melancholy kid regularly gets A's and B's. If she gets an A-, she's depressed. "Oh, I didn't get a perfect score."

Whatever your child's temperament, try to identify it, accept the strengths and weaknesses that it brings, and, most of all, let that child know you love him just the way God created him.

Teach Your Child That He Is Valuable

Many loving parents make the mistake of giving their children the impression they don't measure up. Condemnation, recrimination, and faultfinding tell your child that you wish he were different. Some parents even verbalize their disapproval. You can imagine what that does to a child's self-esteem.

Imagine little eight-year-old Johnny looking up at Mom and Dad with big, liquid eyes, pleading, "Please love me, as I am."

"Shouldn't you be doing your homework?" you ask impatiently.

All you can think about is, *How will he ever get accepted into college if his grades don't improve? Only God could make anything good out of him.*

He turns away slowly, thinking, *If my parents don't think I'll ever amount*

to anything I guess I never will.

That's why it is so important to give our approval and love unconditionally — with no strings attached. Sure, correct their mistakes and the things they do wrong. But always tell them, "I believe God is in the manufacturing business, and He can take your unique gifts and talents and use them for His glory."

Always remember, God has a wonderful plan for your child's life.

Teach Your Children That God Answers Prayer

One of the principles that Bev and I taught our children was that Almighty God is interested in every detail of their lives. We did this not only by studying God's Word together but also by living it.

One Christmas Bev and I were visiting with my married daughter and her family. While walking through the kitchen, I noticed a bulletin board, where they had posted prayer requests. Down in the right hand corner was a picture of a blue Jeep Cherokee.

I knew they'd been having trouble with one of their cars, and that it was time for a new one. When I saw that picture, I couldn't help but laugh. My mind raced back 20 years when our daughter was young.

On our prayer board, we had posted a picture of a red Plymouth station wagon. With four kids, two parents, and neighbor kids going to Sunday school, our family needed the biggest car we could find. At that time, it was the nine-passenger station wagon. I found one in a magazine, and we began praying.

I had been teaching my kids, "In all your ways acknowledge Him, And He shall direct your paths" (Prov. 3:6). In other words, God will supply all your needs. "Knock, and seek, and ask," I told them. After praying for two months, the kids began to think God wasn't listening.

Then one Thursday night — I'll never forget it — the phone rang. It was a deacon from a Baptist church 35 miles across town. I'd never met him, but he worked with a man from our church who knew about our transportation problem. The deacon said, "I understand you're looking for a new car."

"How did you know we were looking for a car?"

When I said "car," the whole house shut down. Every ear tuned in to that conversation.

"I'm in the Navy," he told me, "and I'm being shipped back

to Virginia Beach. I have a car I want to sell."

"Well," I began, "I must tell you right up front, I don't have any money for a down payment."

He said, "That's okay, I just need somebody to take over the payments."

"Well, I'm limited on how much I can spend," I replied "We could only afford $100 a month."

"My payments are $105."

Now, I was interested! "What kind of a car is it?"

"It's a Plymouth station wagon."

My throat went dry, and it was so quiet in the house that I found myself holding my breath.

"How many seats does it have?"

I knew Plymouth also made a two-seat station wagon.

"It's a nine passenger, three-seat station wagon."

Then I really got nervous and asked, "What color is it?"

Long pause. Then he said, "Pastor LaHaye, I almost didn't call you because knowing that you're a minister, I didn't think you'd want a red one."

"A red one!" I shouted, and the whole house went wild.

We rushed over there, did all the paperwork, brought the car home, and all six of us sat in the driveway as we dedicated that car to the Lord.

We enjoyed that station wagon for seven years. In fact, when our kids think back on their childhood, they think of that family car.

Twenty years go by, and my daughter and her family need a car, and so what do they do? Put a picture on the prayer board, believing that God watches and He hears.

Not long after that visit I called my daughter and said, "I'm coming in to San Diego. Would you come by and pick me up at the airport?"

"Sure, Dad, what time are you coming?"

I said, "4:30."

"Oh, good, the kids want to see you when you see it."

I said, "Oh, what is it?"

"I can't tell you. I'm sworn to secrecy."

Guess what "it" was? A blue, four-wheel drive Jeep Cherokee.

Let me ask you a question. Do you think my grandkids think God answers prayers? We've taught them to pray for cars, motorcycles, college, jobs, houses — everything. Why? So their joy can be full, just as God promised (John 15:11).

Teach Your Kids the Secret of Happiness

Parade magazine polled thousands of teenagers and asked them what they most wanted in life. The largest number — 28 percent — said their first desire was happiness; second was a long and enjoyable life. Those two together come to almost 50 percent. The teens' third desire was for marriage and family.

What about a great career? You know, what are you going to do with your life? Surprisingly, that goal ranked only sixth.

Everyone wants happiness.

Happiness is the result of obeying God's principles. How do I know? Because the Bible tells me so.

The psalmist David said, "Happy" or "blessed are the undefiled in the way, Who walk in the law of the Lord!" (Ps. 119:1). Jesus said, "Blessed are those who hear the word of God and keep it!" (Luke 11:28). "If you know these things," — His principles — Jesus said, "blessed are you if you do them" (John 13:17).

Who are the happiest people in the world? The rich and famous? I think not. The self-seekers live in abject misery. God created man morally conscious and responsible to be a servant. It is not the masters but the servants who enjoy happiness. If you serve God, He will bless your life.

Jesus said, "Give, and it will be given to you" (Luke 6:38). Happy is the individual who gives. Show me a giver, and I'll show you a person who accepts himself. He doesn't have an identity crisis. Why? Because he's not worried about his identity. His focus is on others.

If you are a born-again Christian, I hope you can say that you are, with the apostle Paul, "A servant of God and an apostle of Jesus Christ" (Titus 1:1). If you can say that, you are ready to live, and you'll be happy. That doesn't mean you won't have trouble. Let's face it, we're still on planet Earth. You will be able, however, to look to God for the resolution of your problems and be satisfied in investing yourself.

The humanist's world view offers no hope: "When you're dead, you're dead. That's it." The Christian, however, sees this world as a temporary residence, a field that is white unto harvest.

We want to serve Christ by reaching people with the message of salvation as Jesus commanded us: "Go into all the world and preach the gospel" (Mark 16:15). That goal gives us a lifetime motivation and a purpose for living.

The biblical worldview is one of hope that offers life after death. Jesus said, "I go to prepare a place for you. . . . I will come again and receive you to Myself; that where I am, there you may be also" (John 14:2-3). What a wonderful hope!

When we die, we live! And we go to a much better place. Best of all, Jesus will be there. Who could ask for anything more? That's the most important principle your children will ever learn.

Your Best Gift to Your Children

During the 25 years I pastored in San Diego we had a tremendous youth program, an outgrowth of the ministry of Jerry Riffe, who served with me for 23 years, and other youth pastors. We estimate that about 300 young people answered the call of God to go into some kind of Christian work during those years.

After I resigned and before I left, I asked Jerry what kind of homes the Christian workers came out of. He replied, "We have three kinds of homes in our church." Then he listed the following:

1. Spirit-filled families most of the time, and the majority come from these homes.
2. Carnal Christian homes — they almost never come out of those families.
3. Unsaved or mixed, where only one parent was a Christian — they sometimes come out of these families."

I challenged him on that, thinking as pastors do that regular church families, yes, even Christian leader's families would produce better fruit than mixed or unsaved families.

"No," he said, "if Dad is unsaved and acts like a pagan at home, the kids can understand. But if he is a leader in the church and acts like a pagan at home, that is hypocrisy. Young people can't handle that! Which is why they rarely if ever come from such families and go into Christian work."

The best thing you can give your mate and your family is a Spirit-filled mother and father — it will affect their entire life!